To Karin

From Shelby, ♡

Sylvia

Thanx for all your support!

TEACHERS ARE SPECIAL

A TRIBUTE TO THOSE WHO EDUCATE, ENCOURAGE & INSPIRE

COMPILED BY

NANCY BURKE

GRAMERCY BOOKS

New York

This book is dedicated with love, admiration, and awe
to everyone who teaches and everyone who learns.
carpe diem

This 1998 edition is published by Gramercy Books®, a division of
Random House Value Publishing, Inc., 201 East 50th Street, New York, New York 10022.

Gramercy Books® and colophon are registered trademarks of Random House Value Publishing, Inc.

Random House
New York • Toronto • London • Sydney • Auckland
http://www.randomhouse.com/

Interior design: Joan Sommers Design, Chicago
Interior illustrations: Ruta Daugavietis

Printed and bound in Singapore

Library of Congress Cataloging-in-Publication Data
Teachers are special : a tribute to those who educate, encourage & inspire / compiled Nancy Burke.
p. cm.
Originally published: New York : Park Lane Press, 1996.
ISBN 0-517-20264-6
1. Teachers—Quotations. 2. Teachers —Anecdotes.
I. Burke, Nancy, 1949–
LB1775.T377 1998
371.1—dc21   97-32797
                                                                                          CIP

8 7

Credits: Grateful acknowledgment is made to the Swedenborg Foundation for permission to reprint a portion of
Light in my Darkness, by Helen Keller/Revised by Ray Silverman, Chrysalis Books, Imprint of the Swedenborg
Foundation, West Chester, PA, copyright © 1994 by Ray Silverman. All rights reserved.

Acknowledgments

This book would not exist without the extraordinary help and enthusiasm of some outstanding educators, teachers, parents, and students.

Deborah Maher, principal of South Road Elementary School in Kingston, Rhode Island, not only opened up her school to me but personally wrote to several other principals across the country, asking them to help me with the project. Among them was Cynthia List, principal of Jane Addams Vocational High School in the Bronx, New York, who wholeheartedly responded. So too did Evelyn Hassay, second-grade teacher at Cape May Elementary School in New Jersey, who shared wonderful letters, artwork, and reminiscences with me and encouraged several other teachers at her school to participate. Jan Webb, Julie Whitcomb, Mary Horton, and Diane Kern—all teachers at South Road Elementary—really got their classes involved and gave me a great deal of support and encouragement. Patricia Herrity, in New York, tried to get her local school to participate and when that fell through came up with something just as wonderful—the incredible letter written by her son, John, that begins the book. I am indebted to all these women and cannot thank them enough.

My heartfelt thanks also to my editors at Random House, Kate Sheehan Hartson and Lavonne Carlson-Finnerty, who keep me in work and provide inestimable support and guidance.

A very special thank you must also go to Valerie and Gary Cruickshank, who helped out by taking care of my daughter, Katie—along with their own two, Sandy and Bonnie—during the last crunching days of the book. They also

3

gave me much-needed (by then) encouragement by reading some of the manuscript and loving it.

Thanks to the students at Cape May who shared their letters and drawings with me. You're terrific! And a great big thanks to each and every student at South Road—all 460-plus of you—for giving up your recesses and snack times to listen to me talk about the book and for sharing with me your thoughts, ideas, and enthusiasm. I'm sorry I couldn't include all of you.

Finally, my deepest thanks to the students at Jane Addams in New York and particularly to those of you in Mr. Polanco's English class. Your letters touched my heart like nothing has in a long time. More than that, you give me great hope for the future. And to Mr. Polanco: Thank you for doing more than the job description; thank you for not only teaching our children but for caring about them—sometimes when no one else will; thank you for safeguarding our future. Bravo!

4

About the Author

Nancy Burke is a writer and a freelance editor. Her first book, *Meditations on Health: Thoughts and Quotations on Healing and Wellness,* was published by Random House. She lives with her daughter in New England.

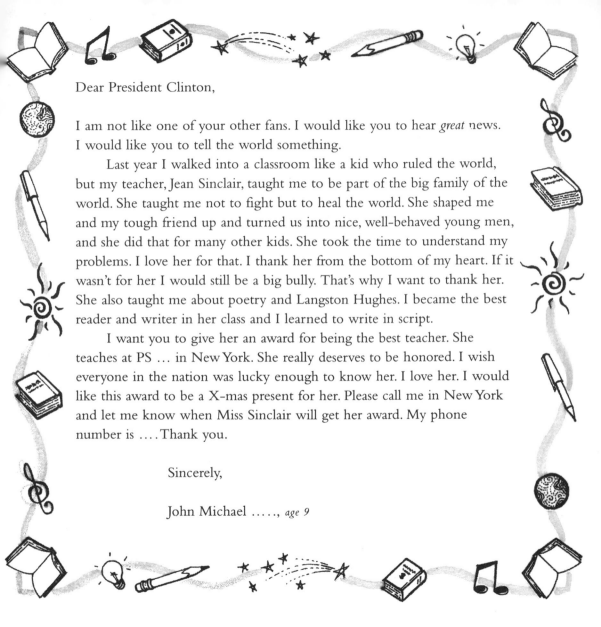

Dear President Clinton,

I am not like one of your other fans. I would like you to hear *great* news. I would like you to tell the world something.

Last year I walked into a classroom like a kid who ruled the world, but my teacher, Jean Sinclair, taught me to be part of the big family of the world. She taught me not to fight but to heal the world. She shaped me and my tough friend up and turned us into nice, well-behaved young men, and she did that for many other kids. She took the time to understand my problems. I love her for that. I thank her from the bottom of my heart. If it wasn't for her I would still be a big bully. That's why I want to thank her. She also taught me about poetry and Langston Hughes. I became the best reader and writer in her class and I learned to write in script.

I want you to give her an award for being the best teacher. She teaches at PS ... in New York. She really deserves to be honored. I wish everyone in the nation was lucky enough to know her. I love her. I would like this award to be a X-mas present for her. Please call me in New York and let me know when Miss Sinclair will get her award. My phone number is .... Thank you.

Sincerely,

John Michael ....., *age 9*

Stuff for a Good Teacher

1. Loves her kids.
2. Helps you out.
3. Always has a smile.
4. Is fair with her kids.
5. Is full of surprises.
6. Takes good care of us.
7. Has smart brains.
8. Tries her best.
9. Likes to laugh.
10. Listens to her heart.

—ALLISON, *age 7*

One looks back with appreciation to the brilliant teachers, but with gratitude to those who touched our human feelings.

—CARL JUNG, *Swiss psychologist*

A teacher who can arouse a feeling for one single good action . . . accomplishes more than he who fills our memory with rows on rows of natural objects, classified with name and form.

—JOHANN WOLFGANG VON GOETHE, *German poet and dramatist*

My English teacher will always have a very special place in my heart. He was there for one of my close friends when she needed comfort. He really helped her out a lot. And he helped me too, at the same time, because he showed me that there are still teachers who care about their students, who are willing to take time out of their busy schedules to help another person, who don't think that the world revolves only around them. I thank him very much for being there for my friend and me, and for showing us the real meaning of the word "Life." It's nice to know there are teachers who haven't forgotten what teaching and love are all about. We will be grateful to him all our lives.

—NAOMI, *age 17*

The mediocre teacher tells. The good teacher explains.
The superior teacher demonstrates. The great teacher inspires.

—WILLIAM ARTHUR WARD, *English novelist*

Everywhere, we learn only from those whom we love.

—JOHANN WOLFGANG VON GOETHE, *German poet and dramatist*

One good schoolmaster is worth a thousand priests.

—ROBERT G. INGERSOLL, *American orator*

We lov'd the doctrine for the teacher's sake.

—DANIEL DEFOE, *English novelist and journalist*

Mr. Hardy always made schoolwork fun. He loved to play around and make jokes. But he wouldn't play at all if you got on his bad side and didn't work. All he wanted to do was teach. And all he wanted us to do was be the best we could be. He told us if we wanted something we would have to work very hard to get it. He told us the real world was tough, that it was hard out there. But he also said, "Don't let anybody tell you you can't make it in life. You can." He would tell us that every day. He cared. That's the best kind of teacher.

—CHRISTINA, *age 15*

Above all things we must take care that the child, who is not yet old enough to love his studies, does not come to hate them and dread the bitterness which he once tasted, even when the years of infancy are left behind. His studies must be made an amusement.

—MARCUS FABIUS QUINTILIANUS, *Roman rhetorician*

One woman who really inspired me wasn't a teacher but a counselor in a junior high school program I used to be in—the AIDP (Absent Improvement/Dropout Prevention). She would talk and talk to me and try to encourage me to come to school every day. She talked to me so much and she was always there to help me do the right thing. My attendance improved a lot. I think that if there were more people like her in the school system, there would be less dropouts.

—DESIREE, *age 17*

Every age has a kind of universal genius, which inclines
those that live in it to some particular studies.

—JOHN DRYDEN, *English poet and dramatist*

. . . that is what learning is. You suddenly understand something
you've understood all your life, but in a new way.

—DORIS LESSING, *English novelist*

If we succeed in giving the love of learning, the learning itself is sure to follow.

—JOHN LUBBOCK, *English financier and author*

Many people would sooner die than think. In fact they do.

—BERTRAND RUSSELL, *English philosopher and social reformer*

Education is not filling a pail but the lighting of a fire.

—WILLIAM BUTLER YEATS, *Irish poet and dramatist*

Thoughts are energy. And you can make your world
or break your world by thinking.

—SUSAN TAYLOR, *American journalist*

The children of this world are in their generation
wiser than the children of light.

—NEW TESTAMENT, LUKE 16:8

The important thing is not so much that every child should be taught,
as that every child should be given the wish to learn.

—JOHN LUBBOCK, *English financier and author*

Train up a child in the way he should go;
and when he is old, he will not depart from it.

—OLD TESTAMENT, PROVERBS 22:6

I love Ms. Webb because:

1. She likes me.
2. She's nice.
3. She's cool.
4. She's funny.
5. She's very kind.
6. She helps you.
7. She takes care of you.
8. She listens to you.
9. She's awesome.
10. She's NUMBER ONE!

—DANIEL, *age 6*

Ms. Webb is friendly when you get to school. She never really
gets mad at you. And she always loves a new kid. I love you Ms. Webb!

—KATIE, *age 7*

Ms. Webb teaches me. She reads with me. She helps me spell
some words. She makes me happy.

—MAE, *age 6*

I like teachers to be nice and sweet and cool and to let us do
our own stuff, and to be kind, really kind.

—MEAGAN, *age 7*

The whole art of teaching is only the art of awakening the natural curiosity of
young minds for the purpose of satisfying it afterwards.

—ANATOLE FRANCE, *French novelist, poet, and critic*

The best teacher, until one comes to adult pupils, is not the one who
knows most, but the one who is most capable of reducing knowledge
to that simple compound of the obvious and the wonderful which
slips into the infantile comprehension. A man of high intelligence, perhaps, may
accomplish the thing by a conscious intellectual feat. But it is vastly easier to the
man (or woman) whose habits of mind are naturally on the plane of a child's.
The best teacher of children, in brief, is one who is essentially childlike.

—H. L. MENCKEN, *American journalist*

Give a little love to a child, and you get a great deal back.

—JOHN RUSKIN, *English writer and critic*

Those that do teach young babes
Do it with gentle means and easy tasks;
He might have chid me so; for, in good faith,
I am a child to chiding.

—WILLIAM SHAKESPEARE, *English playwright,* Othello

I love my teacher. She is nice. She loves her kids. She tells us stories.
She is just so kind. Actually, the number one rule is to be kind.

—CATHY, *age 7*

My second-grade teacher was like a friend, not a teacher. She changed me a lot.
I'm smarter and I'm more aware of things because of her. If she ever needed
anything, I would get it for her. THANK YOU MRS. T!

—JUSTIN, *age 10*

No one has yet fully realized the wealth of sympathy, kindness, and generosity hidden in the soul of a child. The effort of every true education should be to unlock that treasure.

—EMMA GOLDMAN, *Russian-born American lecturer and activist*

Some people are molded by their admirations, others by their hostilities.

—ELIZABETH BOWEN, *Irish novelist*

A child cannot be taught by anyone who despises him,
and a child cannot afford to be fooled.

—JAMES BALDWIN, *American writer*

Level with your child by being honest.
Nobody spots a phony quicker than a child.

—MARY MACCRACKEN, *American writer and art consultant*

Study, learn, but guard the original naïveté. It has to be within you,
as desire for drink is within the drunkard or love is within the lover.

—HENRI MATISSE, *French painter*

My fifth-grade teacher was like a sister to us. She was like a big teenager. She talked like one and dressed like one too. She even liked the same cartoons that we did. And if anyone had a problem, she was right there to fix it. But there was never any trouble in her class. If you tried to start any trouble, you would have to deal with her. She would make you write a punishment assignment for about 100, maybe 1,000 times, depending on what you did. A lot of people changed their ways after all that writing. When the citywide tests were coming up, she was on our behinds every single day. Just to make sure that we knew everything that had been taught to us from the first day on. When we took the citywide tests, everyone in the class passed. That made her so happy. Now that I'm in the ninth grade, I wish I could see her again. Just to thank her for all she did for me.

—DENISE, *age 15*

14

Don't set your wit against a child.
—JONATHAN SWIFT, *English satirist*

For where is any author in the world
Teaches such beauty as a woman's eye?
Learning is but an adjunct to ourself.
—WILLIAM SHAKESPEARE, *English playwright,* Love's Labour's Lost

My English teacher was a sweet nice lady in her mid-20s. She supported me and pushed me to get those high grades. It was beyond just a teacher and her student. We had a friendship. I could talk to her and tell her anything. And she always told me positive things, like how to reach my goals, you know, stuff like that. I am grateful to have met such a nice teacher like her because the image I used to uphold for all teachers was that they were strict and mean and old, ugly-looking people.

—MICHELLE, *age 14*

'Tis pleasing to be school'd in a strange tongue
By female lips and eyes—that is, I mean,
When both the teacher and the taught are young,
As was the case, at least, where I have been;
They smile so when one's right; and when one's wrong
They smile still more.

—LORD BYRON, *English poet*

Charming women can true converts make,
We love the precepts for the teacher's sake.

—GEORGE FARQUHAR, *Irish dramatist*

My special teacher kind of acts like my mother. Like she says if I don't eat she'll tell on me. Maybe she's more like a sister. Anyway, I give her more kisses than anybody else. And she can be funny, too, like when she talks about her boyfriend. She says that he buys her diamond earrings. Yea. Right.

—RYAN, *age 8*

My favorite teacher was my pre-one teacher. Anytime I was upset she'd cheer me up. And when we had a field trip and my mom was supposed to come but never did, my teacher said, "That's okay. I'll pretend to be your mom."

—ERIN, *age 11*

We expect teachers to handle teenage pregnancy, substance abuse, and the failings of the family. Then we expect them to educate our children.

—JOHN SCULLEY, *American business executive*

Teachers who educate children deserve more honor
than parents who merely gave them birth; for bare life
is furnished by the one, the other ensures a good life.

—ARISTOTLE, *Greek philosopher*

The child learns more of the virtues needed in modern life—of fairness, of justice, of comradeship, of collective interest and action—in a common school than can be taught in the most perfect family circle.

—CHARLOTTE PERKINS GILMAN, *American feminist and writer*

The truth of it is, the first rudiments of education are given very indiscreetly by most parents.

—SIR RICHARD STEELE, *English essayist and dramatist*

My mom was an elementary teacher before she married and raised five daughters. In many ways, she was my favorite teacher because she always guided me in the right direction. During my rebellious teen years, my mom tried to save me from the ways of the world. She failed. And I fell over to the dark side. When I matured, she welcomed me back and began teaching me again. Because of her patience, understanding, and positive view of life, I developed into a strong, functional woman—and I became a teacher myself. Thank you, Mom, for teaching, guiding and giving me the tools to have a successful life on this Earth.

—MARY H., *second-grade teacher*

Making the decision to have a child—it's momentous. It is to decide forever to have your heart walking around outside your body.

—ELIZABETH STONE, *American author*

Parents are the bones on which children sharpen their teeth.

—PETER USTINOV, *English actor and playwright*

The joys of parents are secret, and so are their griefs and fears.

—FRANCIS BACON, *English philosopher and essayist*

If you bungle raising your children, I don't think whatever
else you do well matters very much.

—JACQUELINE KENNEDY ONASSIS, *American editor*

My grandmother and my mother are my best teachers. And they taught me well:
to stay out of trouble, to have good manners, and to be a gentleman. They are
strong women and they are both always there for me whenever I need them.
They are my role models.

—WILLIAM, *age 15*

I choose to talk about my mother for three reasons: we have a good relationship,
she wants the very best for me, and she will never let me down. She is always
trying to lead me in the right direction. We're the best of friends and it's that
relationship we have that makes her so special. I'm so glad she's around to see me
grow, mentally and physically, and to help me along the way.

—JAY, *age 16*

I would say that my big sister, Janet, is my favorite teacher. If I have any problems, she helps me out. And she also tells me how the world really is. She tells me a lot about what people do to each other and what I *shouldn't* do. I've learned a lot from her.

—SOL, *age 16*

I believe that anyone can be a teacher, if they are able to touch us, the future of tomorrow, and inspire us to touch someone else's future. A teacher can even be the person who shows you how to tie your shoelaces. One teacher who has given me great inspiration and whose words have made me feel important, special, needed, and intelligent, is my proud father, Eloy. My father wasn't able to finish fifth grade because he had to drop out and work, to help his mother bring in money. But he had this urge to learn and to have an education. So he bought all kinds of books and started educating himself. Now, if you had a conversation with my father, you would think he had graduated from college. It would probably take more than ten papers to describe how my father has influenced me, how he has helped me become the person I am today, how he has helped me find myself. He is just so important and special to me. I will never be able to repay him for what he has taught me—and what he still teaches me, because you never stop learning. So if you are reading this, Dad, I would like to say: Thank you and I love you. What you have taught me will be put into action very soon. You have not wasted your time.

—AIDEE, *age 17*

To nourish children and raise them against odds is in any time, any place, more valuable than to fix bolts in cars or design nuclear weapons.

—MARILYN FRENCH, *American writer*

Mrs. Shelley was choosing a school for her son, and asked the advice of this lady, who gave for advice, "Oh, send him somewhere where they will teach him to think for himself!" Mrs. Shelley answered: "Teach him to think for himself? Oh, my God, teach him rather to think like other people!"

—MARY WOLLSTONECRAFT SHELLEY, *English writer,*
in Matthew Arnold's Essays in Criticism

Man is the only one that knows nothing, that can learn nothing without being taught. He can neither speak nor talk nor eat, and in short he can do nothing at the prompting of nature only, but weep.

—PLINY THE ELDER, *Roman writer and scientist*

Don't limit a child to your own learning, for he was born in another time.

—RABBINICAL SAYING

The true teacher defends his pupil against his own personal influence. He inspires self-trust. He guides their eyes from himself to the spirit that quickens him. He will have no disciple.

—AMOS BRONSON ALCOTT, *American teacher and philosopher*

The object of teaching a child is to enable him to
get along without his teacher.

—ELBERT HUBBARD, *American writer*

I hear and I forget.

I see and I remember.

I do and I understand.

—CHINESE PROVERB

Every man who rises above the common level has received two
educations: the first from his teachers; the second, more personal
and important, from himself.

—EDWARD GIBBON, *English historian*

My third-grade teacher was the best. She made sure I learned. She
taught me right from wrong. And she kept me out of trouble. She told
me to be a leader, not a follower. And that's what I've done. She gave
me pride and self-confidence. She made me understand what life is all about and
how important it is to plan your life. Today I believe in myself. And I'm never
going to let her down.

—DAVID, *age 16*

Follow the path of the unsafe, independent thinker. Expose your ideas to the dangers of controversy. Speak your mind and fear less the label of "crackpot" than the stigma of conformity. And on issues that seem important to you, stand up and be counted at any cost.

—THOMAS J. WATSON, *American businessman*

Learning is not attained by chance, it must be sought for
with ardor and attended to with diligence.

—ABIGAIL ADAMS, *American writer*

The great end of learning is nothing else but to seek for the lost mind.

—MEG-TZU, *Chinese philosopher*

A little learning is a dangerous thing.
Drink deep, or taste not the Pierian spring:
There shallow draughts intoxicate the brain,
And drinking largely sobers us again.

—ALEXANDER POPE, *English poet*

I wake to sleep, and take my waking slow.
I feel my fate in what I cannot fear.
I learn by going where I have to go.

—THEODORE ROETHKE, *American poet*

One teacher who made a big impression on me was my fifth-grade teacher. When I first got to her class I thought the work was too hard. I didn't think I'd even make it to the sixth grade. I was scared. But she taught me not to be afraid. She told me that I was an intelligent girl, and all I had to do was put my mind to the work. With her I discovered I had something I never thought I had—STRENGTH! Now I know I can do anything and be anything. And I will succeed.

—SABREEN, *age 15*

He who learns must suffer. And even in our sleep pain that cannot forget falls drop by drop upon the heart, and in our own despair, against our will, comes wisdom to us by the awful grace of God.

—AESCHYLUS, *Greek playwright,* Agamemnon

He who would leap high must take a long run.

—DANISH PROVERB

Ah, but a man's reach should exceed his grasp
Or what's a heaven for?

—ROBERT BROWNING, *English poet*

My fourth-grade teacher will always be very special to me. She made us work hard, but she made it seem like fun. She always took the time to explain things and she always understood when we did something wrong. She especially helped me during the CAT tests. When I did not understand a part she would just stand there, right by my side, until I got it. When the last day of school came, I asked her if she was going to go on to the fifth grade with us, but she said she was staying in the fourth. When I got home that day, I went up to my room and started to cry. I'll never forget her.

—KELLY, *age 11*

Even though it was a long time ago I can still remember my third- and fourth-grade teacher. I still remember her exact words to me: "You're smart. And I know it and you know it. You can be anything you want to be if you just put your mind to it." She kept on pushing me to do better and try harder. I still see her today and she still gives me lectures but I don't mind. I know I need to be pushed. And I need to hear everything she has to say.

—ANGELICA, *age 16*

When you wish to instruct, be brief; that men's minds take in quickly what you say, learn its lesson, and retain it faithfully. Every word that is unnecessary only pours over the side of a brimming mind.

—CICERO, *Roman orator and philosopher*

We have learnt that nothing is simple and rational except what we ourselves have invented; that God thinks in terms neither of Euclid nor of Riemann; that science has "explained" nothing; that the more we know the more fantastic the world becomes and the profounder the surrounding darkness.

—ALDOUS HUXLEY, *English novelist and critic*

All human wisdom is summed up in two words—wait and hope.
—ALEXANDRE DUMAS PÈRE, *French playwright and novelist*

My second-grade teacher had a big impact on my life. You will say I was too small and I couldn't know what I'm talking about but I will *always* remember what she told me. The first time she saw me she told me that she had a strong feeling about me and that out of all her students, she knew I was one of the ones who would make a real difference in people's lives. And every day she would tell me that if I just kept at it, just kept going the way I was going, I could go as far as I wanted to. I didn't understand her so well back then. But now, when I think back, I know she was right, and I *know* I *can* make it. She was the best teacher I ever had. And I thank her.

—JACITA, *age 17*

Aristotle was asked how much educated men are superior to
the uneducated: "As much," said he, "as the living are to the dead."

—DIOGENES THE CYNIC, *Greek philosopher*

Nobody can be taught faster than he can learn. . . . Every man that has ever
undertaken to instruct others can tell what slow advances he has been able to
make, and how much patience it requires to recall vagrant inattention, to stimu-
late sluggish indifference, and to rectify absurd misapprehension.

—SAMUEL JOHNSON, *English writer and critic*

Don't despair of a student if he has one clear idea.

—NATHANIAL EMMONS, *American theologian*

The teacher should never lose his temper in the presence of the class. If a man,
he may take refuge in profane soliloquies; if a woman, she may follow the
example of one sweet-faced and apparently tranquil girl—and go out in the yard
and gnaw a post.

—WILLIAM LYON PHELPS, *professor of English, Yale University*

Never give up and never give in.

—HUBERT H. HUMPHREY, *American politician*

I am writing this letter about my favorite teacher, Ms. Johnson. She is my fifth-grade teacher. She is wonderful. She is inspiring. She is great. When we don't understand something, she will keep teaching and teaching and teaching until we get it. I don't think any of my teachers has done that before. She is also very neat and organized. Everything has its place. The room is never a mess. All my other teachers were very unorganized. My mom says she likes Ms. Johnson too because this year, I really understand what's being taught. I want everyone to know how WONDERFUL Ms. Johnson really is.

—LAUREN, *age 11*

Education is hanging around until you've caught on.
—ROBERT FROST, *American poet*

I love my teacher. She is the best teacher in the whole world. All she does is sit at her desk most of the day, but I don't care.
—ASHLEY, *age 8*

Know thyself.
—PLUTARCH, *Greek essayist, inscription at the Delphic Oracle*

Because these wings are no longer wings to fly
But merely vans to beat the air
The air which is now thoroughly small and dry
Smaller and dryer than the will
Teach us to care and not to care
Teach us to sit still.

—T. S. ELIOT, *American-born English poet*

I am writing this to show my appreciation to my second-grade teacher. She helped me learn Math, English, and Spelling and she was able to teach me things when no one else could. No one has ever gone that far to help me learn something and I will always love her for it.

—BOBBY, *age 11*

My English teacher has made such a difference in my life. He teaches like no other teacher I've known. He really makes us think—not only about school, but about life. He cares so much about us learning. I've never seen a teacher that cared so much. I've learned more in one year from him than I have in any other class I've ever had.

—TIFFANIE, *age 17*

Know then thyself, presume not God to scan,
The proper study of mankind is man.
Plac'd on this isthmus of a middle state,
A being darkly wise, and rudely great:
With too much knowledge for the sceptic side,
With too much weakness for the stoic's pride,
He hangs between; in doubt to act or rest,
In doubt to deem himself a god, or beast;
In doubt his mind or body to prefer;
Born but to die, an reas'ning but to err;
Alike in ignorance, his reason such,
Whether he thinks too little, or too much.
—ALEXANDER POPE, *English poet*

Life is my college. May I graduate well, and earn some honours!
—LOUISA MAY ALCOTT, *American novelist*

Welcome, O life! I go to encounter for the millionth time the reality of experience and to forge in the smithy of my soul the uncreated conscience of my race.
—JAMES JOYCE, *Irish writer*

When you do know something about the reality of the world that those who stand in ignorance do not know, then you can't not educate.
—BETTY POWELL, *African-American feminist and educator*

Great thoughts come from the heart.

—MARQUIS DE VAUVENARGUES, *French moralist*

Life is a festival only to the wise.

—RALPH WALDO EMERSON, *American essayist and poet*

My special teacher is my boyfriend. The reason why I feel that way is because when I don't understand something, he tries so hard to help me understand. And he definitely encourages me about school. He makes sure that I go. He's very smart and he gives me good advice and he never leads me in the wrong direction. *He* may have made a mistake in dropping out of school, but he will never ever let me do the same. He knows he made a mistake and he doesn't want that to happen to me. All he wants for me is the best.

—SIMONE, *age 17*

All growth is a leap in the dark. . . .

—HENRY MILLER, *American novelist*

There is no royal road to learning.

—EUCLID, *Greek geometer*

To throw obstacles in the way of a complete education
is like putting out the eyes.

—ELIZABETH CADY STANTON, *American suffragist*

All want to be learned, but no one is willing to pay the price.

—JUVENAL, *Roman satirist*

Learning is not child's play; we cannot learn without pain.

—ARISTOTLE, *Greek philosopher*

You have learnt something. That always feels at first as if you had lost something.

—GEORGE BERNARD SHAW, *Irish-born British playwright*

The things which hurt, instruct.

—BENJAMIN FRANKLIN, *American statesperson*

Learn as though you would never be able to master it;
hold it as though you would be in fear of losing it.

—CONFUCIUS, *Chinese philosopher*

My sex education teacher, Mrs. Isakson, had the biggest impact on me. She was really more of a friend than a teacher. She was the kind of person you could always come and talk to if you had any problems. She tried to help a lot of kids, kids who wanted to kill themselves, or kids who wanted to hurt someone. Sometimes I felt sorry for her, because it was just so much and some people really took advantage of her. She was someone I could really look up to and respect in every way. I'll never forget her.

—SHANI, *age 14*

No one can make you feel inferior without your consent.
—ELEANOR ROOSEVELT, *American humanitarian*

In the deserts of the heart
Let the healing fountain start,
In the prison of his days
Teach the free man how to praise.
—W. H. AUDEN, *English-born American poet*

Education has really one basic factor, a *sine qua non*—you must want it.
—GEORGE EDWARD WOODBERRY, *American critic and teacher*

To talk in public, to think in solitude, to read and to hear, to inquire and answer inquiries, is the business of the scholar.
—SAMUEL JOHNSON, *English writer and critic*

We should be careful to get out of an experience only the wisdom that is in it—and stop there; lest we be like the cat that sits down on a hot stove-lid. She will never sit down on a hot stove-lid again—and that is well; but also she will never sit down on a cold one anymore.

—MARK TWAIN, *American writer and humorist*

It was in fourth grade that I had my most favorite teacher. He was terrific and understanding. He had a lot of wisdom and he was always doing something nice for the class. When we would sit down with him to go over our papers, he'd always make a game of it. He'd play tic-tac-toe with us, right on our papers. (And I was the first one to actually beat him!) He was a great guy.

—DUSTIN, *age 12*

We have need of very little learning to have a good mind.

—MICHEL DE MONTAIGNE, *French moralist and essayist*

Much learning does not teach understanding.

—HERACLITUS, *Greek philosopher*

Teach the tongue to say "I do not know."

—MAIMONIDES, *Spanish-born Jewish philosopher*

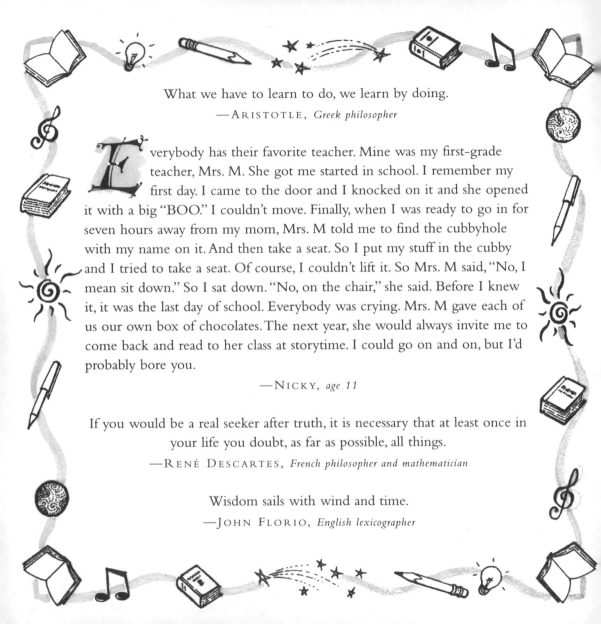

What we have to learn to do, we learn by doing.

—ARISTOTLE, *Greek philosopher*

Everybody has their favorite teacher. Mine was my first-grade teacher, Mrs. M. She got me started in school. I remember my first day. I came to the door and I knocked on it and she opened it with a big "BOO." I couldn't move. Finally, when I was ready to go in for seven hours away from my mom, Mrs. M told me to find the cubbyhole with my name on it. And then take a seat. So I put my stuff in the cubby and I tried to take a seat. Of course, I couldn't lift it. So Mrs. M said, "No, I mean sit down." So I sat down. "No, on the chair," she said. Before I knew it, it was the last day of school. Everybody was crying. Mrs. M gave each of us our own box of chocolates. The next year, she would always invite me to come back and read to her class at storytime. I could go on and on, but I'd probably bore you.

—NICKY, *age 11*

If you would be a real seeker after truth, it is necessary that at least once in your life you doubt, as far as possible, all things.

—RENÉ DESCARTES, *French philosopher and mathematician*

Wisdom sails with wind and time.

—JOHN FLORIO, *English lexicographer*

That alone is liberal knowledge, which stands on its own pretensions,
which is independent of sequel, expects no complement, refuses to be
informed . . . by any end, or absorbed into any art, in order
duly to present itself to our contemplation.

—JOHN HENRY NEWMAN, *English theologian and writer*

Wisdom never lies.

—HOMER, *Greek poet*

Knowledge is recognition of something absent;
it is a salutation, not an embrace.

—GEORGE SANTAYANA, *Spanish-born American philosopher and poet*

No one is ever old enough to know better.

—HOLBROOK JACKSON, *English essayist and editor*

They know enough who know how to learn.

—HENRY ADAMS, *American historian and scholar*

Knowledge is power.

—FRANCIS BACON, *English philosopher and essayist*

Not to know certain things is a great part of wisdom.

—HUGO GROTIUS, *Dutch jurist and statesperson*

The mind is slow in unlearning what it has been long in learning.

—SENECA, *Roman philosopher and playwright*

Education is what survives when what has been learned has been forgotten.

—B. F. SKINNER, *American psychologist*

Men must be taught as if you taught them not,
And things unknown proposed as things forgot.

—ALEXANDER POPE, *English poet*

Knowledge is proud that he has learn'd so much;
Wisdom is humble that he knows no more.

—WILLIAM COWPER, *English poet*

The first and wisest of them all professed
To know this only, that he nothing knew.

—JOHN MILTON, *English poet*

All knowledge is of itself of some value. There is nothing so minute or inconsiderable that I would not rather know it than not.

—SAMUEL JOHNSON, *English writer and critic*

To teach is to learn twice.

—JOSEPH JOUBERT, *French essayist and moralist*

An extensive knowledge is needful to thinking people—
it takes away the heat and fever; and helps, by widening speculation,
to ease the Burden of the Mystery.

—JOHN KEATS, *English poet*

The more we study the more we discover our ignorance.

—PERCY BYSSHE SHELLEY, *English poet*

To accomplish great things, we must dream as well as act.

—ANATOLE FRANCE, *French novelist, poet, and critic*

To think great thoughts, you must be heroes as well as idealists.

—OLIVER WENDELL HOLMES, *American jurist*

The thinkers of the world should by rights be
guardians of the world's mirth.

—AGNES REPPLIER, *American essayist and poet*

My teacher is very special. She helps me out a lot and she is nice to me and she teaches me about stuff and when I first came to her classroom I was afraid of bugs but now I'm not.

—KRYSTEN, *age 8*

My English teacher, Mr. P, had a big impact on me. He doesn't only teach everything there is to know about English, but he also teaches us everything we need to know about life. He shows us how to have fun and learn at the same time. And he never puts us down when we can't accomplish something the first time out. Instead, he helps us start over again. And even when he is in a bad mood, he always finds a way to hide it from us. He tries to cheer us up instead. I think that makes him feel good about himself. It makes me feel good.

—MADELINE, *age 15*

I liked my third-grade teacher the best. She gave us popcorn and movie parties and brought us outside every chance she got. And when we did something bad, she'd always say, "Gee, you did *great.*" Then she would say, "I was being sarcastic." And we'd all start to laugh. (And when we went to lunch, she would get us there *very* early so we wouldn't have to wait in line!)

—JOHN, *age 10*

Without knowledge, life is no more than the shadow of death.

—MOLIÈRE, *French playwright*

Knowledge is the antidote to fear.

—RALPH WALDO EMERSON, *American essayist and poet*

The ideal condition
Would be, I admit, that men should be right by instinct;
But since we are all likely to go astray,
The reasonable thing is to learn from those who can teach.

—SOPHOCLES, *Greek playwright,* Antigone

Example is the school of mankind, and they will learn at no other.

—EDMUND BURKE, *British statesman and orator*

Climb high
Climb far
Your goal the sky
Your aim the star.

—*inscription on Hopkins Memorial Steps,*
Williams College, Williamstown, Massachusetts

Delightful task! to rear the tender thought,
To teach the young idea how to shoot.

—JAMES THOMSON, *Scottish poet*

For rigorous teachers seized my youth,
And purged its faith, and trimmed its fire,
Showed me the high, white star of Truth,
There bade me gaze, and there aspire.

—MATTHEW ARNOLD, *English poet and critic*

My favorite teacher was my second-grade teacher. When we did Science he would help us a lot (because he would always give us the first letter of each answer on our tests). And you didn't get in trouble if your homework was a little late. He was very funny too. When someone came to the classroom door to ask him something, he'd squirt them with a water gun.

—AMANDA, *age 11*

If to do were as easy as to know what were good to do, chapels had been churches, and poor men's cottages princes' palaces. It is a good divine that follows his own instructions: I can easier teach twenty what were good to be done, than be one of the twenty to follow mine own teaching.

—WILLIAM SHAKESPEARE, *English playwright,* The Merchant of Venice

I would live to study, and not study to live.

—FRANCIS BACON, *English philosopher and essayist*

Never seem more learned than the people you are with. Wear your learning like a pocket watch and keep it hidden. Do not put it out to count the hours, but give the time when you are asked.

—EARL OF CHESTERFIELD, *English statesperson and author*

The vanity of teaching often tempteth a man to forget he is a blockhead.

—GEORGE SAVILE, *English statesperson and essayist*

My best teacher was Mrs. A. I was lucky because I had her in kindergarten, second grade, fourth grade, and sixth grade. The thing that was special about her was she helped me with love and with understanding. Not like this other teacher I had, who used to hit me on my head so much that I would go home with big headaches. She finally stopped hitting me when I said I was going to tell the principal. Then she told me she only hit me so that I would learn. Mrs. A was different. She was always trying to get to know us better. And if you had a problem, she was always there for you. Now, that's a real teacher.

—ENEIDA, *age 15*

It might be argued, that to be a knave is the gift of fortune, but to play the fool to advantage it is necessary to be a learned man.

—WILLIAM HAZLITT, *English essayist*

Study is like the Heaven's glorious sun,

That will not be deep-search'd with saucy looks;

Small have continual plodders ever won,

Save base authority from others' books.

These earthly godfathers of Heaven's lights

That give a name to every fixed star,

Have no more profit of their shining nights

Than those that walk and wot not what they are.

—WILLIAM SHAKESPEARE, *English playwright,* Love's Labour's Lost

A professor is one who talks in someone else's sleep.

—W. H. AUDEN, *English-born American poet*

My teacher is special because she never yells at me and she never ever slaps me, and she's never mean to me, and she never ever ever says swears to me. She loves children.

—REBECCA, *age 8*

My first-grade teacher was special to me because I didn't have any front teeth then and I couldn't talk that well and people used to tease me a lot. But she would stick right up for me. I still get teased about the way I talk. I wish she was still here.

—FONTIA, *age 16*

The decent docent doesn't doze;
He teaches standing on his toes.
His student dassn't doze and does,
And that's what teaching is and was.

—DAVID MCCORD, *American writer*

The regular course was Reeling and Writhing,
...and the different branches of Arithmetic—
Ambition, Distraction, Uglification, and Derision.

—LEWIS CARROLL, *English writer and mathematician,* Alice's Adventures in Wonderland

My karate teacher can break 12 bats over his head
and 10 bricks with his bare hands. That's why he's special.

—BILLY, *age 7*

Such labored nothings, in so strange a style,
Amaze th' unlearned, and make the learned smile.

—ALEXANDER POPE, *English poet*

My teacher is fun and hard-working and never forgets to take time to talk to her students, unlike some teachers who only teach and never talk. And she has nicknames for all of us. She calls me "Sugarlips." Of course she is a little absent-minded, but that usually means she forgets when reports are due, which is OK.

—SARAH, *age 11*

To love what you do and feel that it matters—
how could anything be more fun?

—KATHARINE GRAHAM, *American newspaper publisher*

Children should be led into the right paths, not by severity, but by persuasion.

—TERENCE, *Roman playwright*

Go, teach eternal wisdom how to rule—
Then drop into thyself, and be a fool!

—ALEXANDER POPE, *English poet*

Ah God! Had I but studied in the days of my foolish youth.

—FRANÇOIS VILLON, *French poet*

A diller, a dollar,
A ten o'clock scholar,
What makes you come so soon?
You used to come at ten o'clock,
But now you come at noon.

—NURSERY RHYME

But to go to school in a summer morn,
Oh, it drives all joy away!
Under a cruel eye outworn,
The little ones spend the day—
In sighing and dismay.

—WILLIAM BLAKE, *English poet*

My third-grade teacher gave us Popsicles, drinks, and all kinds of snacks, especially when we had a test. She also had lots of games that helped us with Spelling and Math and she always found the greatest books to read. She never gave us a lot of homework. Once, she didn't give us homework for a whole month!

—MARK, *age 11*

My tae kwon do headmaster is special because
he trains our bodies *and* our spirits.

—LUCAS, *age 11*

Any place that anyone can learn something useful from someone
with experience is an educational institution.

—AL CAPP, *American cartoonist*

You can get all A's and still flunk life.

—WALKER PERCY, *American novelist*

y first-grade teacher was special. If we got all of our papers right, she would let us get a piece of candy or a sticker. And she let us bring our pets into school. And one day she brought in some flour and we made homemade bread! She also wants to buy my horse and she said that of course all the money would go to me.

—TOBIN, *age 9*

My basketball coach was the best because he taught me
how to dribble, how to pass, and how to score like a man.

—SAM, *age 10*

My favorite teacher really liked kids. I remember in his class that we would get together in teams and have a big math quiz. The team with the most points got pizza or McDonald's. He also had a great sense of humor and he understood kids and he always helped them out if they had a problem. He told great stories too. He knew how to make hard work seem fun, and fun seem funner.

—SARAH, *age 11*

Theories and goals of education don't matter a whit
if you don't consider your students to be human beings.

—LOU ANN WALKER, *American editor and author*

46

It is paradoxical that many educators and parents still differentiate
between a time for learning and a time for play without seeing
the vital connection between them.

—LEO BUSCAGLIA, *American author and lecturer*

Mix with your sage counsels some brief folly.
In due place to forget one's wisdom is sweet.

—CICERO, *Roman orator and philosopher*

My third-grade teacher was the best. I had him for science and we got to
look at protozoans, coral, sponges, and all different kinds of jellyfish. But my
most favorite thing was that he let us watch a praying mantis eat a cricket.
That was really cool.

—MATT, *age 11*

As plants are suffocated and drowned with too much moisture,
and lamps with too much oil, so is the active part
of the understanding with too much study.

—MICHEL DE MONTAIGNE, *French moralist and essayist*

What will a child learn sooner than a song?

—ALEXANDER POPE, *English poet*

Deign on the passing world to turn thine eyes,
And pause a while from learning to be wise.
There mark what ills the scholar's life assail—
Toil, envy, want, the patron, and the jail.

—SAMUEL JOHNSON, *English writer and critic*

I like my fourth-grade teacher because she helps me understand things, and she explains things very very good. Some teachers talk too fast, but she talks at a good, steady pace. I think she deserves to be treated more nicely than she is. Kids talk back to her and don't do what they are told. I don't do that, of course. I'm nice and do what I'm told.

—DANIELLE, *age 9*

One of my most special teachers was my second-grade teacher. He always read funny books, like *Pickle Lady. Pickle Lady* is a book about a lady who does everything with pickles.

—WILLIAM, *age 11*

In the education of children there is nothing like alluring the interest and affection; otherwise you only make so many asses laden with books.

—MICHEL DE MONTAIGNE, *French moralist and essayist*

Much had he read,
Much more had seen; he studied from the life,
And in th' original perus'd mankind.

—DR. JOHN ARMSTRONG, *Scottish poet and physician*

It is with books as with men: a very small number
play a great part, the rest are lost in the multitude.

—VOLTAIRE, *French essayist and philosopher*

O friend unseen, unborn, unknown,
Student of our sweet English tongue,
Read out my words at night, alone:
I was a poet, I was young.

—JAMES ELROY FLECKER, *English poet and playwright*

I took a speed-reading course and read *War and Peace*
in twenty minutes. It's about Russia.

—WOODY ALLEN, *American actor, writer, and film director*

I would have to say my first-grade teacher was the best. She taught
me to read when I thought I couldn't. It made me feel just so great.

—KAITLIN, *age 8*

There is no frigate like a book
To take us lands away,
Nor any coursers like a page
Of prancing poetry.

This traverse may be the poorest take
Without oppress of toil;
How frugal is the chariot
That bears a human soul.

—EMILY DICKINSON, *American poet*

I remember when my second-grade teacher pushed me and pushed me to read and when I finally started to read I liked it so much I couldn't stop!

—CHRIS, *age 8*

Literature is my Utopia. Here I am not disenfranchised. No barrier of the senses shuts me out from the sweet, gracious discourse of my book friends.

—HELEN KELLER, *American memoirist, essayist, and lecturer*

Learn to read slow: all other graces
Will follow in their proper places.

—WILLIAM WALKER, *American filibuster*

The love of learning, the sequestered nooks, and all the sweet serenity of books.
—HENRY WADSWORTH LONGFELLOW, *American poet*

The true university of these days is a collection of books.
—THOMAS CARLYLE, *Scottish-born English essayist*

Examples draw where precept fails,
And sermons are less read than tales.
—MATTHEW PRIOR, *English poet and diplomat*

Some books are to be tasted, others to be swallowed, and some
few are to be chewed and digested.
—FRANCIS BACON, *English philosopher and essayist*

When I am dead, I hope it may be said:
"His sins were scarlet, but his books were read."
—HILAIRE BELLOC, *English writer*

If you cannot read all your books, at any rate handle them, and, as it were, fondle
them. Let them fall open where they will. . . . Make a voyage of discovery, taking
soundings of uncharted seas.

—SIR WINSTON CHURCHILL, *British statesperson and author*

I was like an unconscious clod of earth. There was nothing in me except the instinct to eat and drink and sleep. . . . Then suddenly, I knew not how or where or when, my brain felt the impact of another mind, and I awoke to language, to knowledge, to love. . . . My teacher, Anne Mansfield Sullivan, had been with me nearly a month, and she had taught me the names of a number of objects. She put them into my hand, spelled their names on her fingers and helped me to form the letters; but I had not the faintest idea what I was doing. . . . One day she handed me a cup and formed the letters *w-a-t-e-r.* She says I looked puzzled and persisted in confusing the two words, spelling *cup* for *water* and *water* for *cup.* . . . In despair she led me out to the ivy-covered pumphouse and made me hold the cup under the spout while she pumped. With her other hand she spelled *w-a-t-e-r* emphatically. I stood still, my whole body's attention fixed on the motions of her fingers as the cool stream flowed over my hand. All at once there was a strange stir within me—a misty consciousness, a sense of something remembered. It was as if I had come back to life after being dead. I understood that what my teacher was doing with her fingers meant that the cold something that was rushing over my hand was water, and that it was possible for me to communicate with other people by these hand signs. . . . That first revelation was worth all those years I had spent in dark, soundless imprisonment. That word *water* dropped into my mind like the sun in a frozen winter world.

—HELEN KELLER, *American memoirist, essayist, and lecturer,* Light in My Darkness

Education is what you learn in books,
and nobody knows you know it but your teacher.

—VIRGINIA CARY HUDSON, *American essayist*

The wise are above books.

—SAMUEL DANIEL, *English poet*

A good teacher, like a good entertainer, first must hold his
audience's attention. Then he can teach his lesson.

—HENDRIK JOHN CLARKE, *American poet, writer, and editor*

The art of teaching is the art of assisting discovery.

—MARK VAN DOREN, *American writer and editor*

What can I say to you? I am perhaps the oldest musician in the world. I am an
old man, but in many senses a very young man. And this is what I want you to
be, young, young, young all your life, and to say things to the world that are true.

—PABLO CASALS, *Spanish-born cellist, conductor, and composer*

My singing teacher is very, very special. She got a voice from God!
And *she* didn't even have to take singing lessons!

—CAREY, *age 9*

I consider a human soul without an education like marble in a quarry, which shows none of its inherent beauties until the skill of the polisher sketches out the colors, makes the surface shine, and discovers every ornamental cloud, spot, and vein that runs through it.

—JOSEPH ADDISON, *English essayist and poet*

To live content with small means; to seek elegance rather than luxury, and refinement rather than fashion; to be worthy, not respectable, and wealthy, not rich; to study hard, think quietly, talk gently, act frankly; to listen to stars and birds, to babes and sages, with open heart; to bear all cheerfully, do all bravely, await occasions, hurry never. In a word, to let the spiritual, unbidden and unconscious, grow up through the common. This is to be my symphony.

—WILLIAM ELLERY CHANNING, *American clergyman*

I must study politics and war that my sons may have liberty to study mathematics and philosophy. My sons ought to study mathematics and philosophy, geography, natural history, naval architecture, navigation, commerce, and agriculture, in order to give their children a right to study painting, poetry, music, architecture, statuary, tapestry, and porcelain.

—JOHN ADAMS, *second president of the United States*

Education is an ornament in prosperity and a refuge in adversity.

—ARISTOTLE, *Greek philosopher*

Look to the Classics, History, to the Arts, for there is the truth.
Look away from the systems, the processes, the techniques.

—CHARLES GUGGENHEIM, *American motion picture-television producer*

Teaching is an instinctual art, mindful of potential, craving of realizations,
a pausing, seamless process.

—A. BARTLETT GIAMATTI, *American educator*

Education is not a *product*: mark, diploma, job, money—
in that order; it is a *process*, a never-ending one.

—BEL KAUFMAN, *German-born American educator and writer*

If you think education is expensive—try ignorance.

—DEREK BOK, *president, Harvard University*

More money is put into prison construction than into schools. That, in itself, is
the description of a nation bent on suicide. I mean, what's more precious to us
than our children? We're going to build a lot more prisons if we don't deal
with the schools and their inequalities.

—JONATHAN KOZOL, *American author and education reformer*

Teachers are expected to reach unattainable goals with inadequate tools. The miracle is that at times they accomplish this impossible task.

—HAIM G. GINOTT, *Israeli-born American child psychologist*

The task of universal, public, elementary education is still usually being conducted by a woman alone in a little room, presiding over a youthful distillate of a town or a city. If she is willing, she tries to cultivate the minds of children both in good and desperate shape. Some of them have problems that she hasn't been trained to identify. She feels her way. She has no choice.

—TRACY KIDDER, *American author*

I didn't really have any special teacher until this year. Then I met some teachers who really care about their students. You see, I had my son when I was 15 years old and it was hard for me because even though I wanted to go to school, I didn't have a baby-sitter. So I was absent a lot. I still did my work. I was determined that I wasn't going to let anyone or anything keep me from my education. But even though I did my work, because I was absent so much my teachers weren't supposed to pass me. They did anyway. I'll never forget them and I thank them all.

—ONHEKI, *age 16*

Human history becomes more and more a race between education and catastrophe.

—H. G. WELLS, *English novelist, sociologist, and historian*

Education is simply the soul of a society as it passes
from one generation to another.
—G. K. CHESTERTON, *English journalist and author*

Education makes a people easy to lead, but difficult to drive;
easy to govern, but impossible to enslave.
—LORD HENRY PETER BROUGHAM, *British jurist and essayist*

The teacher that was most special to me was my seventh-grade teacher. She
was strict, but very understanding and very nice. Everybody paid attention to
her, even the troublemakers in the class. And she once told me something
that I would never forget. She told me that "knowledge is power." Other
people had told me that before, but the way *she* said it made me realize that
she—and everyone who had ever told me that—was right. I will always love
her for that.

—ROSA, *age 16*

By education most have been misled;
So they believe, because they so were bred.
The priest continues what the nurse began,
And thus the child imposes on the man.
—JOHN DRYDEN, *English poet and dramatist*

'Tis education forms the common mind:
Just as the twig is bent the tree's inclined.

—ALEXANDER POPE, *English poet*

Perhaps the most valuable result of all education is the ability to make yourself do the thing you have to do, when it ought to be done, whether you like it or not; it is the first lesson that ought to be learned.

—T. H. HUXLEY, *English biologist and writer*

Why is it today that we seem to be afraid of urging kids on to excellence and achievement? Our society is more inclined to let kids develop at their own pace—not push them too hard.

—RUSH LIMBAUGH, *American social commentator*

Never regard study as a duty, but as the enviable opportunity to learn to know the liberating influence of beauty in the realm of the spirit for your own personal joy and to the profit of the community to which your later work belongs.

—ALBERT EINSTEIN, *German-born American physicist*

I touch the future. I teach.

—CHRISTA MCAULIFFE, *American teacher and astronaut*

My English teacher always has time to listen to his students. And he brings out the best in us. He encourages us to do better, to try harder, and to never give up. Probably the most important thing he taught me—as a Hispanic and a young woman—is that I can be anything I want to be if I get my education and I work hard. The world would be a better place if it were filled with more caring teachers like him.

—JESSICA, *age 16*

The only medicine for suffering, crime, and all the
other woes of mankind, is wisdom.
—T. H. HUXLEY, *English biologist and writer*

The schools of the country are its future in miniature.
—TEHYI HSIEH, *Chinese educator, writer, and diplomat*

If you have built castles in the air, your work need not be lost;
That is where they should be. Now put the foundations under them.
—HENRY DAVID THOREAU, *American essayist and naturalist*

The roots of education are bitter, but the fruit is sweet.
—ARISTOTLE, *Greek philosopher*

I had a teacher in junior high who was incredible. He was always there, talking to us about learning and staying in high school and going on to college. If he heard about us being out in the street, doing something bad and cutting school, the next time he saw us, he'd sit us down and tell us how much he cared about all of us and how much he wanted all of us children to do better. I started to believe that if we didn't show up at school, he'd just stop whatever he was doing in the classroom and come and find us —at one of our houses or in the playground—and drag us back. He was just always *there*. Finally, so was I. Now I'm in the ninth grade, trying my best to get to the tenth grade. And if it wasn't for him, I know I'd be in some friend's house, doing God knows what, and not going anywhere.

—NATASHA, *age 15*

The ability to think straight, some knowledge of the past, some vision of the future, some urge to fit that service into the well-being of the community— these are the most vital things education must try to produce.

—VIRGINIA GILDERSLEEVE, *American activist and statesperson*

All our dignity consists then, in thought. By it we must elevate ourselves, and not by space and time which we cannot fill.
Let us endeavor, then, to think well. . . .

—BLAISE PASCAL, *French mathematician and philosopher*

Dive into the sea of thought, and find there pearls beyond the price.

—MOSES IBN EZRA, *Jewish poet and critic*

Nurture your mind with great thoughts;
to believe in the heroic makes heroes.

—BENJAMIN DISRAELI, *British prime minister, politician, and author*

It is only the ignorant who despise education.

—PUBLILIUS SYRUS, *Latin writer*

Whoso neglects learning in his youth,
loses the past and is dead for the future.

—EURIPIDES, *Greek playwright,* Phrixus

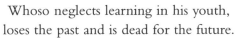

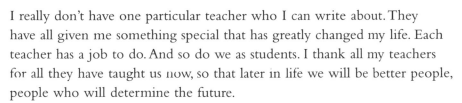

I really don't have one particular teacher who I can write about. They
have all given me something special that has greatly changed my life. Each
teacher has a job to do. And so do we as students. I thank all my teachers
for all they have taught us now, so that later in life we will be better people,
people who will determine the future.

—VANESSA, *age 15*

Come, my friends,
'Tis not too late to seek a newer world....
It may be that gulfs will wash us down:
It may be we shall touch the Happy Isles,
And see the great Achilles, whom we knew.
Tho' much is taken, much abides; and tho'
We are not now that strength which in old days
Moved earth and heaven; that which we are, we are;
One equal temper of heroic hearts,
Made weak by time and fate, but strong in will
To strive, to seek, to find, and not to yield.

—ALFRED, LORD TENNYSON, *English poet, "Ulysses"*

Mrs. H was my favorite teacher. When I gave her flowers, I gave her fake ones because they'd never die on her. Nobody will ever stop me from loving her! And in a 100 years she'll still be as good a teacher as now. Mrs. H, please come back. Brandon is being real bad!

—ALLISON, *age 7*

The years teach much which the days never know.

—RALPH WALDO EMERSON, *American essayist and poet*

I have been teaching for just about thirteen years, and I still feel grateful for this challenging and rewarding profession. Yes, there are many demands on my time. . . . Yes, there is always something new to learn. . . . Yes, many days I come home feeling worried about a troubled child. . . . And yes, every so often I come home "burnt-out." Teaching is not easy. I continue to teach because for me, the art of teaching is all about the beauty of the risk of forming significant relationships. Teaching may be about giving, but it is also so much about receiving. Teaching is a privilege because it is all about touching the lives of children and allowing them to touch mine. Teaching is about caring and wanting and expecting the very best from every child in my class. Teaching is about joy and laughter and singing and playing. Teaching is about growing. As I write this, there are only nine days left in this school year and I realize once again that teaching is also about saying good-bye and letting go. This year's class has been no different than any other: the time we had together has been precious. And so I say good-bye, with wonderful wishes, to: Dan, Emerson, Nick, Katie, Mae, Danielle, Josh, Billy, Joe, Jesse, Sarah, Brooke, Dan, Brian, Michelle, Ashley, Mason, Kenny, Joey, Julie, Ashley, and Alex. Teaching is also about love.

—JAN WEBB, *first-grade teacher*

In teaching you cannot see the fruit of a day's work.
It is invisible and remains so, maybe for twenty years.

—JACQUES BARZUN, *French-born American critic and educator*

It is for us to make the effort. The result is always in God's hands.

—MOHANDAS K. GANDHI, *Indian nationalist leader*

I am a part of all that I have met;
Yet all experience is an arch wherethro'
Gleams that untravell'd world, whose margin fades
For ever and for ever when I move.

—ALFRED, LORD TENNYSON, *English poet*

Lives of great men remind us
We can make our lives sublime,
And, departing, leave behind us
Footprints on the sands of time.

—HENRY WADSWORTH LONGFELLOW, *American poet*